THE LION PRIDE

BY IRYNA COLVIN SPENCER

DEDICATION

This book is dedicated to all the Lions Worldwide, but more specifically to the Lancaster Lions, where I served, and who exemplify the perfect example of what service to the community is all about.

I'm also dedicating this book in honor of the late Lancaster Lions, George M. Colvin.

I'm also dedicating this book to my grandchildren, who loved participating in the Lancaster town parades, and marching with the Lancaster Lions organization.

ACKNOWLEDGEMENTS

I would like to thank my special friends, former Lions Mary and Peter Arena, who were instrumental in my membership to this wonderful, worthwhile, community service-based organization.

Mary was also instrumental in my accepting the position as editor of our Lancaster Lions Club newsletter, which was the catalyst for my expanding my writing career.

A special thank you to my granddaughter Kristin Colvin who did the illustrations for this book.

CHAPTER ONE

INTRODUCTION TO THE LION PRIDE

"Theo, Kayla, please come inside. It's time you were taught about the Lion Pride and the creed by which we abide," Jewel called out to her children.

"Oh brother," Theo said to his twin sister, Kayla. "I can't believe she's calling us in so soon. I thought we were told we had an hour of play time. Here we go again, another lecture about what I did wrong or I am about to do wrong." Theo rolled his big brown eyes at his sister.

"How do you know it's about you? I was called in too! Besides mother said it was about something called the Lion Pride. Isn't that the group of people that she and papa get together with?" Kayla replied, "I'm not happy about this either. I was on my way to Tasha's to try out a new hairdo, and talk about what happened in school today."

Theo, Sr. and his wife, Jewel, waited in the living room. "This can't be good," Kayla whispered. "They want us in the living room. You know, our formal room? The one we call the forbidden room, and that's always a bad sign. Something serious must be up. We are only allowed in there when we have special guests."

As they cautiously approached the living room, they noticed their father was already standing up pacing the floor. They sat down on the coach near their mother, and looked directly at their father. Their way of acknowledging they were paying attention.

"Ahem," Theo, Sr. cleared his throat. "As you know, your Mother, and I are very involved in our community. We would like the two of you involved too. We would like you both to think of some way you help others. Our neighbors and friends have been a big part of our lives, and instrumental in yours. They babysat you when you were younger, and we had commitments we both had to attend. They helped out when your mother and I were sick, and when we had other unexpected emergencies. Now that we are all getting a bit older, your mother and I thought it would be a good idea if we formed a group that was informed about what was happening in our neighborhood, and give a helping hand when we can."

"But papa," Theo interrupted. "Is it really that important that we help out? We are very young, what can we possibly do?"

"It most certainly is important," his father replied. "As senior members of our Lion Pride, we must teach our cubs about being compassionate towards our neighbors, assisting them when we can. There are so many ways we can help. Both of you can decide which of your friends you would like to invite to join us in this endeavor. After all, if we all work together it will give you that much more time to spend with your friends. Together there is so much more we can do to help others. We can mow lawns, do yard clean up, rake leaves,

shovel snow, run errands, or just provide companionship to our neighbors. Some of our neighbors have diminished vision, and would love to
have stories read to them. Some of our neighbors
have no family members left, and are lonely. Just
spending some time with them would brighten
their day."

Their mother interjected with "We can also fix dinners, bake cookies and pies, clean their homes, do laundry, maybe babysit their young cubs so that they can get out and do some errands, or anything else they can't do with their children around. All we have to do is remember that we are doing this for people we love and care about."

With big eyes, both cubs looked at their father, and Kayla asked, "Papa, you always tell us to be careful, so how can we just stop by anyone's house alone? Isn't that just the opposite of what you taught us?"

Theo looked at his young children, smiling as he did so. Evidently his children had paid attention to his previous warnings, and he was pleased that they heeded his advice. "You would never go to anyone's house alone. We are called the Lion Pride for a reason. We go as a group to help. There is always someone in the community who finds out about our neighbors who may need help, or are in trouble. More often than not, people don't like to broadcast their problems, but may let something slip up in the course of their conversation with a close neighbor, or another family member. Or, someone may over hear the conversation about to their neighbor's misfortunes. Your mother and I would first call or visit our neighbor in need. When we arrive, we will look around and observe for ourselves what may need fixing. During the course of our visit we can find out what their needs might be. Afterwards we can organize a committee to take care of all the things that may need attention. For example, Lion Geo is a plumber, and he can take care of any water problems. Lion Peter is a carpenter, and he will make any repairs in the home that need attention. Lion Geno is an all-around handy man, and can fix almost anything. Lionesses Maraya, and your mama are excellent cooks and bakers. Lions Bette and Mike are organizers. They can look at the list of problems, and set up schedules to get things repaired or taken care of, depending on the size of the problems. We can also prepare some meals so that the family doesn't go hungry. We can assist with any household chores. Collectively, we can do just about anything."

"That's really cool," Theo said, "and I sure do like going over to Lioness Maraya's home. She makes the best cookies, and she always gives me chocolate milk to go with them."

With a glance at his mother, he added, "Mother, I like your cookies, too."

Kayla chimed in, "I can help with doing dishes, dusting, babysitting, and taste testing, of course. Lioness Loren always seems grouchy and has piles of dishes in her sink. She is always so mean. Do we have to help her, too?"

"Kayla, Lioness Loren is a little bit older, and suffers from a lot of aches and pains. That's why she appears to be grouchy. She lives alone, ever since her husband passed away. Since they did not have any cubs, I can imagine she may be lonely too. It would really be a big help to her if we went over there to help with the dishes and anything else that she needs done, things that she can no longer do for herself." Jewel looked at her daughter hoping that her daughter would grasp what she just told her.

"Maybe if we help out, they will give us some money or something?" Theo asked.

"Now, now, children, you are not doing this for any money. You are doing this because we are good neighbors, and good neighbors help each other," Papa said.

"That's right," Jewel interjected. "We, as a family, could go visit some of our neighbors who are in nursing homes. Many of the residents in those homes no longer have families, or any-one else visiting them, and they get lonely. They sometimes need someone to talk to, share their stories with, and to laugh with. We go there to help them feel better. We could also learn a lot from them. For instance, what they did when they were young. Many of them led interesting lives, and would just love sharing their stories with anyone who will take the time to listen. So often I have walked away feeling just a little bit better because I made somebody's day brighter. I know I always feel better about myself when I can help someone out." Jewel smiled as she finished that statement, remembering the last elderly lioness she had visited. She recalled the smile on her face and the big hug she received from her when she left.

"Would that be like when we spent time with our Grammy and Grandpa and they told us about the olden days?" Kayla asked. "Grandpa told us about fighting in the war so that we could be safe. Grammy told us how she met Grandpa after the war, and then they got married."

"Yes, it would be similar." Jewel smiled.

"So, okay. If we do all those things, you just mentioned, what do we get?" Theo asked.

"Well," both parents chimed in, in unison. "You go first, papa," Jewel purred.

"What you get is a sense of pride knowing that you did your best to brighten somebody's day. You get big smiles, a hug, and sometimes they will share some cookies and candy with you."

Jewel added, "Not only that, but when you leave, you feel good about yourself. You gave them something to look forward to."

"What will they have to look forward to?" Theo asked. As Jewel reached over to give them both a big hug, she replied, "Another visit from you," she said with a smile.

"But how can our Lion Pride do so much?" Theo asked. "It's easy" Jewel said. "We don't do it all by ourselves. We form groups with some of our neighbors. We each get to choose which type of job we are better at. With more Lions pitching in and working together, we can do so much more in a lot less time."

"So, it's all about the groups, and working together?" Kayla asked.

"Absolutely," Jewel replied. "The groups can consist of new, and old friends, and neighbors. Every time we work together, we forge new friendships. Sometimes, when we get together, we come up with other ways we can help our neighbors. We find out what our neighbors' needs are. Many times, just by observing and listening. More often than not, people don't like to complain or ask for help. Their inner pride keeps them from asking for assistance."

"Like when Cullen told us in school that their daddy was really sick, and their mommy had to go back to work?" Theo asked.

"Yes, just like that," Jewel replied. "You came home and told us, and before the end of the day, we called everyone in our pride, and started a meal chain to make sure the family was fed."

"Another example," papa said, "was when the ambulance took Lion Harold to the hospital? We all became aware that he had a medical problem. We know he lives alone, and someone had to feed his pets and take care of his garden. I let him know there was nothing to worry about. I told him the lion pride would take care of everything. When Lion Harold came home, he saw that everyone pitched in, and completed the repairs around the house, prepared meals and cleaned for him. The smile on his face was more than enough payment. That is what this is all about, being in a community that becomes more like an extended family."

Kayla and Theo listened with interest. "Can we get our friends to help, too?" Kayla asked.

"Absolutely," Jewel replied. "If Tasha and Peyton, or any of your other friends want to help, they would be most welcome. Remember, you are never to go to anyone's home alone to help out. There must always be an adult present. We go as a group, and work together to get everything done. You, Tasha, and Peyton could watch the little cubs, and you might be able to help with some dusting or minor cleaning jobs. Theo and his friends could help out with yardwork and clean up. Papa and I are hoping that you could talk to your friends and find out which ones would be eager to help. This will not only give your more time to spend with your friends, but it will also be quality time."

"When do we start?" Kayla asked.

Theo Sr. looked lovingly at both his cubs. The hair around his neck fanned out with pride, as he observed the willingness of his cubs to help others. He smiled over at Jewel, and could see that she was emotionally touched as well. "Well, my children, we are truly pleased that you are so eager to help out. First you have to contact your friends, and bring us a list of all those willing to help. Your mother and I will do the same. Once we have a list of willing participants, we will put that list together as to everyone's availability. We don't expect that everyone will always be able to help out, but if we have an idea what days are good for them, it will be easier to put plans into place. What we are doing is volunteer work. Some of our neighbors who want to help out hold full time jobs, and can't always participate. Some of our neighbors are limited to what they can do because of their own physical limitations, but still want to help out. We can put those neighbors on phone duty, where they can contact the other neighbors with schedules that we come up with. The same situation may apply to your friends," he said with a smile, as he glanced over at his cubs.

"Your mother and I will sit down after this meeting and put down a list of names of neighbors we will be contacting to join us at our home next week to put our plan into action. We would appreciate it if you would do the same, and provide us with a list of names of all your friends you think would like to help out. We will then go over with them what we are thinking of doing, and ask them for any suggestions they may have. People love it when they are included, it gives them a feeling of being needed, which they are. So now," he said looking at his family, "Let's get to it."

CHAPTER TWO

FORMING THE LION PRIDE

Theo Sr, Jewel and the cubs got busy the next day contacting all their friends and neighbors, and gave them a brief idea what the meeting at their house the following week would be all about. They asked them to think about what they would like to contribute to this neighborhood effort. Everyone they spoke to seemed really eager to help out.

The following week they were overwhelmed by the turnout. Everyone they had spoken with showed up for the meeting. It ended up being a pot luck gathering, with everyone bringing a dish to pass.

Theo Sr. stood up, and cleared his throat to talk. He looked around the room, and with a big smile on his fact greeted everyone. "Thank you all for coming to this gathering. Judging by the amount of food that is here, we can stay together for at least a week." There was laughter around the room, as everyone shook their head.

"As you all know," Theo began again when the laughter subsided, "we are all getting on in years. Some more than others. We find that we cannot accomplish the repairs that we one could. Truthfully, I cannot bend, get down or get up as fast as I once could."

"Maybe some exercise would help," Lion Dan shouted out laughingly. He and Theo were good friends for over twenty years, and often golfed together.

Theo laughed and replied, "Yes, it just might, but unfortunately that would take some time to get me back into shape. However, you all know where I'm coming from. We just can't do all the things we once could. There have been times when we have had to help each other on a one-to-one basis, but that's because we all know each other well enough to do that. It's easy for us to lien on each other without feeling guilty. I'm sure you know of other neighbors, and friends who are not comfortable asking for help. They need it, they just don't know how to ask for it, or whom to ask to get it. That's where we come in. I've given this matter plenty of thought for some time now. Jewel and I have discussed it often. I know from speaking to some of you that this same thought has crossed your mind. So, instead of just talking about it. Let's do something about it. That's why we asked you here today. You are all among the most caring, and loved family and friends we are proud to know. Your hearts are in the right place. You care about your family, friends, your neighbors, and our community. What I would like is some suggestions from you on what we can do to help out those in our community in need."

Lion Mick suggested hosting a pot luck dinner once a month for anyone wishing or able to attend. Then if we have some left over food donate it to those in the community who were unable to attend. This way letting them know that we are thinking of them, and missed them. Everyone agreed that was a great idea.

Lion Peter suggested that we contact some of our elders to see if they could use a hand with sprucing up their homes, by painting the inside or out, doing any internal repairs that didn't require a contractor's license. He indicated that he had overheard a few of the elderly in our population lamenting about things that needed repair that they could not do themselves anymore, but also couldn't afford to hire anyone. Lion Gene chimed in that he too would be willing to help out, and would accept any volunteers that are willing to pitch in.

Lioness Maraya said she would be more than happy to occasionally provide meals, and desserts, and would also head up any committee that would like to get involved in that endeavor. She said that way we could have a food chain. One of the Lionesses said that they could set up schedules so that one of them would be responsible for each day of the week. Then, if one of them couldn't take their turn, or was unavailable, they could rely on another Lioness to take their turn. That way each day was covered. A lot of the Lionesses agreed that was a great idea, and already started planning meals that could be frozen until needed.

They all agreed that setting priorities would be necessary for those in the community needed immediate assistance.

The young cubs listened intently to what their parents and neighbor were talking about. Theo Jr. said he had an idea where they could help. "We talked among ourselves, and came up with some ideas. We would be happy to help with cutting the grass, weeding, since we have to weed by hand, there are plenty of us to help out."

"Why do we have to weed by hand?", his friend John asked.

"Well," Theo, Sr. chimed in, "we don't use any chemicals on our plants or our lawns. Therefore, we do everything by hand, and we have garden tools that help make our jobs easier. It's nice to hear that my son has been paying attention to me when I was working with him in our garden," he smiled over at his son.

Theo, Jr. continued, "We can also rake leaves, and put them into piles. We can help with snow shoveling, feeding and walking their pets. There are so many things we would be willing to help out with.

Kayla jumped up and added, "Yes, we were all talking in our circle too about all the ways we could help out. We can babysit, help feed the babies, read to them, and play with them if it would help their parents to other things around the house. We could also help out with the pets. We also wouldn't mind helping out with the baking, and we all agreed to be taste testers." She said the last part with a smile at her friends. They all sat there nodding their heads.

"What about going to the nursing home to see the grandma's and grandpa's that can't walk or see anymore?" Kayla asked. "Can we go visit them? I could read to them, or sing for them. I can even show them my new dance. Wouldn't that be fun?"

"Definitely. We can even take them some of our homemade cookies, Kayla, but it is okay if you don't sing. The nursing homes do not encourage any loud noises in case some of the lions are sleeping." Jewel said laughingly. She smiled with the knowledge that, while her daughter could belt out a tune, however, she was tone deaf. Not wanting to discourage Kayla from singing, she thought it was best to let her know that silence is golden.

The evening was drawing to a close. Lion Mick and Lioness Betty agreed to be the organizers, and would work with the committee chairs to assure that things ran smoothly.

Lioness Maraya took over the food preparation committee, with most of the Lionesses and young girl cubs signing up to help out.

Lioness Jewell and Tanya took on the compassionate committee. That committee was responsible in giving some care to those community members that became ill. If they didn't have family members, they would see to it that the proper health care was obtained for them. This committee was also in charge of arranging for companionship and, baby-sitting duties. They had quite a list of volunteers, and advised those on the list that they would rotate all of them, so that no one would be called on more than once a week.

Lions Peter and Gene agreed to co-chair the home improvement committee, which consisted of painting, and doing minor repairs around the house.

Lions Dan and Theo agreed to co-chair the outside gardening committee. They looked around and smiled broadly at all the young male cubs that were willing to help out.

Lion Theo stood up and walked into the center of his living room, turning around to everyone with a big smile. "I don't know where to begin to thank you all for coming. You not only agreed to volunteer, but exceeded our expectations of what Jewel and I had envisioned when we planned this. Actually, both of us had thought who might take the leadership rolls, and we just about had it right. We didn't expect this overwhelming gathering, and cannot tell you how much love, and heartfelt gratitude we have for all of you. Please remember this is a volunteer group, and if you have priorities in your own life, those should always come first. What we learned here today, and what we imparted to our young cubs is, it doesn't matter how young or how old you are. It doesn't matter how big or how small you are. We all have something special to contribute, and that is what makes us the Lion Pride."